Travels with Ted

by Jay Brown

SECOND EDITION

**Phonetically controlled to the
Wilson Reading System®**

Wilson Language Training Corporation

www.wilsonlanguage.com

Travels with Ted (Steps 1-6 B)

Item # TWT-JB

ISBN 978-1-56778-043-1

SECOND EDITION (revised 2004)

The Wilson Reading System is published by:

Wilson Language Training Corporation
47 Old Webster Road
Oxford, MA 01540
United States of America

(800) 899-8454

www.wilsonlanguage.com

Printed in the U.S.A.

February 2006

Foreword

The vocabulary in Travels with Ted is selected to provide practice in developing decoding skills. The story is intended for students in junior high school, high school or adult education programs. The word structure follows the structured language sequence of the Wilson Reading System. However, the phonetically controlled text will be useful to all emerging readers.

Chapter

1 Closed syllables, one syllable words without blends (WRS step 1.6)

2 Closed syllables, one syllable words with blends (WRS step 2)

3 Multisyllabic, closed syllable words (WRS step 3)

4 Multisyllabic, closed and vowel-consonant-e syllable words (WRS step 4)

5 Multisyllabic, closed, v-c-e & open syllable words (WRS step 5)

6 Suffixes are added to unchanging basewords and consonant-l-e syllables are added in the final pages (WRS step 6)

There are some words that do not fit the structured language sequence. Without them, a story cannot be written, at least one with any semblance of flow. These words should be learned as sight words before the reader embarks on **Travels with Ted**. These words are:

a	**the**	**and**	**of**
he	**she**	**to**	**was**
for	**or**	**her**	**they**
were	**are**	**be**	**no**

Additionally, an occasional, exceptional word (an outlaw) may be included in the text. When it is, it will be in **boldface** type. These words may be read for the student (if they are not known) since they do not fit into the phonetic patterns that have been taught.

To all the special people, young and old, who struggle with words

Memorized Words

Step

1	the, a, he, me, we, she, and, is, was, his, to, of, I
2	so, go, be, my, by, they, her, for, or, you, your, from
3	would, could, should, said, how, now, some, come, what, do
4	their, very, were, why, Mr., Mrs., Ms., only, want, are, says, there
5	goes, does, where, who, again, against, one, two, four, put, pull, push, full
6	about, often, once, any, many, gone, done, none, answer, has, always
7	become, four, sure, people, friend, father, been, woman, hour, minute
8	special, animal, purpose, both, usual, together, love, move, prove, above
9	February, Wednesday, enough, route, though, beauty, walk, talk, lose, aunt
10	through, young, laugh, police, machine, heart, month, blood, sugar, ocean
11	thought, shoulder, double, trouble, court, although, material, color, length, strength
12	imagine, restaurant, medicine, thorough, iron, half, cousin, million, couple, library, chocolate, guarantee

Additional Memorized Words

approval, change, control, curtain, earl, fashion, fountain, heard, learn, liter, marina, mountain, obey, onion, pearl, prove, resource, rough, tomb, touch, tough, whole

Travels with Ted
by Jay Brown

CHAPTER ONE

Ted **lived** with his mom and dad in Webb Hill, **Maine**. His mom had a lot of hens in a shed up on the hill. When Ted was six, his mom let him mix the mash for the hens. He fed them the mash and got the eggs for his mom. Then he sat in the shop with his mom to sell the eggs. That was fun.

Ted's dad ran a box mill. His dad had his men cut logs for the **boxes**. Then it was Meg's job. Meg ran the BIG CAT to lug the logs to the mill. The men in the mill then **made** the logs **into boxes**. When Ted was a kid, his dad let him sit up in the cab of the BIG CAT with Meg. That was fun.

When Ted was ten, his dad had him fill in at the box mill. His dad had him run odd jobs and mop up. That was not much fun. But then his dad let him cut logs with the men. Ted was ten, but he was big for ten, and he did the job of a man. In the mill his job was with the box lids. He had to set a lid on the top of a box, tap it to fit well, and then fix a WEBB HILL MILL tag on the lid.

Ted was with his dad at the mill for ten **years**. It was not a bad job, and his dad was not a bad boss. His dad did not nag him and did not yell at him. The gals and men he met at the mill were his pals. But it was a dull job and Ted was fed up with it. When he was **twenty** he had a big fuss with his gal. He had a yen to run off and sop up a bit of sun.

With that he quit the job.

His dad had a fit when Ted quit the job. He **said** Ted was a nut to quit. But Ted was not a kid. It was his wish to quit and that was that. He was a man, and his mom and dad had to let him get his wish. It was sad for them, but they did not bug him.

Ted had a yen to get on a bus and run off. He had the cash for the bus, and he **could** get odd jobs to fill in the gaps when his cash ran thin. His mom was not mad but was sad and did sob a bit. She got in a big fuss to fill a **lunch** box for him on the bus: buns with lox, ham and jam, chips and cans of pop. Ted had a hug for his dad, a kiss for his mom, and a pat for his dog Shep.

They all had to rush off in the van to get Ted to the bus. His dad had a map and a bit of cash for him. Ted's cap fell off in the van, but he was in such a rush to get on the bus he did not miss it. When the bus was all set to rev up, Ted had to get off to get his cap. His dad ran to the van to get it. Then, with his cap, cash, **lunch** box, and bag, Ted got on the bus and was off.

On the bus Ted had to tag his bag and toss it in the bag bin. He had his box of buns and pop with him. Ted sat with a thin **boy** and a big man with a red wig. The **boy** had a big tin box on his lap. He did not chat much, but lit up when Ted **gave** him a bun with jam. He **said** he was Sam Ross and that he was ten.

He had a pet fox in his big tin box. It was a kit fox that he had dug up **from** a fox den. An egg man shot the **mother** fox that got in his shed to kill his hens. When Sam dug up the kit fox, it was ill fed and thin. His dad **said** he had to kill it and get rid of it, but Sam fed it and had it as his pet. He was on this bus with the fox to **see** a vet in Bath.

When Sam had his fill of buns, he had a nap. Then the tin box fell off his lap with a thud, and the lid fell off. The kit fox ran at the leg of the big man and had a nip at his cuff. The man had such a fit that his red wig fell off. The wig fell on the fox, and the fox ran off with the red wig. The **people** on the bus set up a yell to **see** that big ball of red fuzz on the run.

The fox with the red wig hid in a box of fish on the bag rack. It was a mess. Sam got up and ran with his cap to the box of fish. At last he got the fox in his hat. He put the fox, with a bit of the fish, in his tin box. The red wig was wet with fish. The big man was mad. He got his wig, but he did not put it on.

From then on the bus trip was dull.

CHAPTER TWO

Ted and Sam got off the bus at Bath. Sam ran off to the vet with his pet fox. Ted was a bit sad. He had a pang for his mom and dad and Shep. He did miss them and the gang at the mill. He was sunk and at a loss in Bath. But it was not all that bad. He was well fed and had a bit of cash. He rang the bell at the bus **depot** and had the man tag his bag and fit it in the bin. When he got rid of the bag, he did a hop and a jig, sang a song, and set off on the long path to the **harbor**.

At a pub in the **harbor** he met Hank, a kid from Bath. Hank had a job at the bank but was off for lunch. He and Hank got on well. Hank was a whiz at ping-pong and had set up a net on a big **table** in the back of the pub. They had fun at that. Then they got bits of fish at a fish shop to toss to the gulls on the wing. That was fun, but when a fish chunk hit slam bang on the deck of a big tank ship, he and Hank had to quit. The man on the ship was mad that he had to get that gunk off his ship. At the top of his lungs he **said** he **would** sic his dog Fang on them if they did not quit. Thank God he did not. Then Hank had to rush off to the bank.

Ted had to think of a bunk and a peg to hang his hat for the **night**. He set off on the long path up the hill to the bus stop.

When Ted got to the top of the hill, he sat on a bench to plan his next step. To Ted, Bath was big, with its ships and shops. He felt lost in the thick of things. He was stiff and hot from the long bus trip, and he did wish so much for a dip in the spring-fed pond at Webb Hill. Just then a bunch of kids in swim trunks ran past. Ted got them to stop to ask **where** he **could** swim. The kids **said** he **could** swim at the Swank Swim Club up the hill. That **would** cost him a lot of cash, and Frog Pond was just as much fun. Then the kids **said** to bring his stuff and swim with them. With that Ted sprang up, got his bag from the man at the bus stop, and in a flash dug his swim trunks from his bag. He left his bag at the bus desk, and went off with them to Frog Pond.

Next to the pond was a log hut **where** Ted **could** slip on his trunks. He hung his pants and things on a peg in the hut and ran off for a dip in the pond. The sun was hot and the pond was fresh and chill. He had fun with the kids. He **would** swim to the raft with them, jump off, and then flop flat on the raft to bask in the sun. It was lots of fun **until** Ron Kemp fell.

Ron was a small child, not as old as most of the kids. A wet plank on the raft let him slip, and he fell. He hit his leg on the raft and got a mild bump and a gash on his shin. The cut bled a lot, but Ted got a soft pad to press on it and told him to hold it till he **could** bind it with his belt.

At the end of the swim Ted had a long chat with the kids in the sun. At dusk, the bugs got bad, and he went to the log hut to dress. Ron had a limp from his fall on the raft, and he felt punk. Ted went with him to find his mom and dad. The Kemps

could not thank Ted **enough** for his kind help to Ron. They pled with Ted to stop a bit with them. They had a glass of punch with chips and small snacks. Ted fed the Kemp's cat a pan of milk. From then on the cat sat in his lap and was his best pal.

When, at last, Ted got up to go, the Kemps pled with him to stop with them for the **night**. They **would** not let him go to the inn. They told him he had to help Ron and tend to that cut shin. A fresh cot was set up for him in the loft. They told Ted they were his hosts, and he was to mind them. They got his bag from the bus stop. Then they fed him and sent him off to the loft. Quick as a wink the cat ran up to the loft with him. The **night** was cold, but for most of the **night** the cat was snug in the folds of the bunk with Ted.

With his long bus trip and the swim with the kids, the thing Ted had in mind was a long rest. His fond wish was to flop on a soft bed. It was not long till he did drop off. He slept well, but then sat up with a gasp when he felt the press of cold, damp flesh on his chin. It was just the soft kiss of his old pal the cat. Ted did his best to toss the cat off the bed, but it clung to him. He felt he had to nod off and get his rest, but that wet kiss on his chin kept him up.

At last Ted got up. The sun was not up. It was not yet six. He got his things on and sat in the chill loft. The cat sat on his lap, but Ted was mad and fed up with that cat.

When the Kemps got up, Ted left the loft and met Ron and his dad to chop and split logs. A brisk cold snap had left a thin crust of frost on the grass and a skim of **ice** on the duck pond. It was a cold task as a blast of wind swept the land. Ted got an ax to help with the job and help lug the logs to the shed. When Ted got the ax, the cat ran off and left its path of soft prints in the frost. With the logs split and in stacks, Ted and Ron and his dad went in for brunch. When Mom Kemp fed the men she did not scrimp. She had set up a grand brunch: eggs and grits with thin strips of crisp ham, hot buns with plum jam, and a jug of fresh, cold milk. At the end of brunch, Mom Kemp swept up the crusts and scraps to toss to the ducks in the pond.

Ron was a kind of wild kid and was apt to sprint and jump a lot. When he did, the gash in his leg bled. To get him to hold still, Ted **made** a splint of split sticks and folds of soft felt. To bind it to Ron's leg, he had to strap it on with long strips of cloth. Ted told them to hold it on till the leg got well.

It was just ten when Ted left the Kemps. He was glad that he had met them, but he had to get on with his trip. It was kind of them to let him bunk in the loft. He did thank them and felt he **would** miss them all. All but the cat.

CHAPTER THREE

The Kemps had given Ted a snug bed in the attic and had fed him well. They were kind to him, and it was with sadness that he left them. He felt sad, but he was glad to get on with his trip.

From the Kemps he went to the bus stop. A brisk wind had sprung up and his thin cotton top was not much help in the cold. He set his bag on the top of a trash basket and dug into his bag for his jacket. When he shut the bag and went to lift it, the bottom of the bag hit a snag on the trash basket. With a sudden rip, the bottom split and his things fell on the grass. It was comic stuff for a TV channel but not for Ted. It was not a fun thing to happen, and Ted was upset and in a panic. He did not relish the fact that all his things were on the grass for the public to discuss. Ted swept up his things, and his bag went into the rubbish. Then he went to The Camp Shop and got a canvas duffel bag. It cost him a lot, but he had to get it to finish the trip. He was glad that his dad had given him a bit of cash when he left Webb Hill. With his things in the duffel bag, he went to the inn for a muffin and a glass of milk, and to plan his next step.

He had to admit that this step of the trip was not much fun.

Ted sat in the inn with his muffin and his duffel bag. His mind was on his trip, but he did happen to spot at the inn desk:

BELLHOP JOB

ASK AT DESK

The cost of the duffel bag had put a dent in his wallet, and he felt it best that he get a job. He went to the desk and rang the bell. A man met him to discuss the job and told him it was for just seven **days**. The past bellhop was ill with a common cold and bad tonsils. The job of the bell-hop was to lug bags and trunks from the van or bus to the inn. He had to fill in on odd jobs as well: polish the brass, dump the baskets into the ashcan, dust, and run small trips within the inn. But most of the job was to help admit the **guests** to the inn and tend to them.

For the job, Ted got bed and **board** and a small sum of cash from the inn. It was the custom for **guests** to tip the bellhops, and all the tips he got were his. His bed was in the annex next to the inn, and he got his **meals** in the annex with the rest of the help. Ted was glad to get the job. It was not a bad setup: bed and **board** for seven **days** and cash as well. Things were on the upswing. He went to find his bed in the annex.

All of a sudden, Ted was a bellhop.

As a bellhop, Ted had to dress in red denim pants and a red pillbox cap. He was not to chitchat or hobnob with the **guests**. He had to hop up when the bell rang to summon him to the desk. Ted did not mind the bags and trunks. He was big and fit. The job with his dad in the box mill had given him strong legs and calluses on his hands.

Ted met all kinds of **guests** at the inn.

An old gal spent her visit at the inn with her lap dog Button. Ted fed Button and kept it in the kennel. He got a lavish tip for this but had to admit he had fun with Button. A bishop was at the inn on his visit to the Bath chapels. A drunk sang unfit songs when the Chess Club had a banquet, and Ted had to expel him from the inn. The big man with the red wig, the man Ted had met on the bus, was at the inn. He got a lavish tip from an old man with a gunshot blast in the hip from **World War II**. The man was from **London**. He met bigwigs and common men. It was seldom dull at the inn.

At the end of the seven **days**, the man **who** ran the inn told him he had a spot for him on the staff. Ted had to think **about** that. At last, Ted felt he would set off on his trip and not **stay** at the inn. He did finish with a fat **wallet** and lots of things to tell.

When Ted was a bellhop at the inn, men told him of tall ships and of travels to distant lands. One man with a **bronze** suntan told him of the tranquil, sunlit tropics. When he left the inn, he set off on the gravel path that led to the **harbor** at the bottom of the hill. In the **harbor there** were vessels of all kinds, from ships with tall masts to small skiffs.

Ted sat on a bench. He saw a gull flap its wings, spin and twist, then plummet into the **water**. It would vanish with a splash to bring up a fish in its bill. Ted sat on the bench for a long **time**. On land he saw men bend **down** to mend nets. He saw **others** with a shovel and basket to dig for clams in the sand.

Of all the ships in the harbor, one cast a spell on Ted. Pennants and flags hung from its tall masts. There was a brass **signal** bell on its cabin. The hull of that ship was spotless. It had a splendid emblem of a gold dragon on it. That ship enchanted him, and he had the wild wish to get on it. His big problem was the cost. He was restless and **dismal**, and went into the pub for a sandwich and a cold drink.

Ted was sad as he went into the Scottish Pilgrim Pub. He had a strong wish to get a trip on that ship, but there was a limit to the things he could expect to do. He had to admit he could not spend his cash on such lavish things. He had to dismiss the trip on the ship to distant lands. He felt he was a victim of his **wallet**. It was a sad lesson, and it upset him. He was glum and sullen as he went into the pub.

In the pub, he left his duffel bag in a closet and went to get a sandwich. He sat in a dim end of the pub next to six men from the ships. **One** of the men had a red cap; on it was the emblem of a golden dragon. He told the **others** that he was frantic to find a man to help on his ship the next day. All of a sudden, Ted had a plan. He did not want to disrupt the men at that instant. He kept to himself, but when, at last, they did disband, he went to the man in the red cap to discuss the prospect of a job. Ted told the man that he **would** be glad to enlist on the ship for a **day**.

The man in the red cap was Big Jim Buskin. It did happen that he was in command of the Golden Dragon. A man on his ship had a sudden illness, and Big Jim was frantic. He had a contract with a class of children from the public **schools** for a **cruise** on his ship the next day. He had to find a strong adult to assist him on the cruise, to rig the ship and trim the canvas, and to attend to the children as well. He was to run the ship up the channel to Mullet Sands and let the kids off to swim and picnic on the sand flats. The Golden Dragon was to set off from the **harbor** at ten A.M. and would expect to finish the trip at the **harbor** at seven P.M.

Ted was a bit timid, but he was on the level. He told Big Jim the biggest channel he had **been** in was his bathtub. He had to admit he could not tell canvas from linen. Ted felt he **would** be a misfit on a ship but **would** attempt to do his best. Big Jim told Ted he **could** instruct him, and that most of the job was to attend to the children. He had a hundred bills for Ted if he **would** help on the **cruise**. That did it; Ted **would** go.

Ted got his duffel from the closet, and they went to visit the Golden Dragon for a lesson on ships. Big Jim led him to a bunk on the ship, and Ted slept snug and content. He got his wish for a **cruise** on the Golden Dragon.

Ted was up at six. If he was to be the assistant to Jim on the **cruise**, he felt he had to accustom himself to the ship. To him the Golden Dragon was an enchanting ship. It had fantastic rigging that ran from the hull to the top of the tall mast. The **sails** were of thin cotton or a kind of plastic cloth. The wall panels in the cabin of the ship had a fresh shellac finish, and the brass had a splendid polish. A grand magnetic compass was set on a pedestal in the cockpit. Big Jim got on the ship with a set of lessons for Ted in the rigging of the **sails**. Ted had a strong wish to establish himself as a **sailor** on the Golden Dragon. He did not want to discredit himself to Jim. But the exotic rigging, the vast **sails** and the splendid compass were all novel to him. He was mistrustful of his skill for the job. Jim was an old **sailor** and could set and trim the **sails** himself. He did not tell Ted this; he **would** let Ted fret a bit. Ted's big job was to be attendant to the children. Big Jim did not **want** to do that. A **school** bus was to bring the children to the dock, and Ted was to collect them and bring them to the Golden Dragon.

The sun was up, the wind was mild and constant. One **could** expect a tranquil **cruise**.

Big Jim's cruise for children was just **one** segment of a vast, non-profit project run by the public **schools**. The object of the project was to let children travel at minimal cost to enrich and expand their **lives**. It attracted children of all ethnic **cultures**, **ages** six to twelve. Big Jim **expressed** his willingness to enlist in the project and conduct a **cruise** for the children on his Golden Dragon.

The bus got to the dock at ten A.M. and let off a frantic throng of expectant children. They had an astonishing bunch of stuff for the **cruise**: sunglasses, fishing rods, nets, caps, and picnic baskets. It was a distressing mishmash until Ted got them in **line**. At last he led them to Big Jim Buskin and the Golden Dragon. Big Jim had to impress upon them that he was commandant of the ship. He was insistent that they mind him. He went on to establish the plan for conduct on the ship, and told them that misconduct **would** be met with punishment. With this, the children were given **life** vests and sent up the gangplank onto the Golden Dragon. Ted told the kids to stop the jumping and handsprings, but it was such a thrill for them that they could not stand still.

Big Jim set the **sail**, got in the cockpit with his magnetic compass, and cast off for a **sail** into the Atlantic.

The **cruise** to Mullet Sands was fun, but Ted **could** not accustom himself to the lift and fall of the ship and had a bit of gastric distress. The children had no problem and were ecstatic with the crashing of the hull in the big **waves**. They clung to the ship's **lines** and let the splash of the **waves** dampen them with **salt spray**.

When they got to Mullet Sands, Big Jim sat in the cabin and sent Ted to fulfill his commitment with the children. Ted and the kids went off with blankets to set up the picnic encampment.

It was a devilish job tending to the children! Ted had to enlist the help of the big kids, but all of them were a bit wild. With tactfulness and a strong will, all went well. Ted set up a badminton net, and they had athletic contests with ball and bat and with a plastic **frisbee**. Most of the kids swam. They went on a hunt to collect crabs, scallops, clams, mussels, and shells. One of the gals got sand in her egg salad sandwich and **another** one got cut on a jagged fragment of glass. That did not diminish the fun much. All in all, it was a splendid day, and the kids were unwilling to end it. At last Ted collected them all and got them on the ship. On the **cruise** to the **harbor** they sang songs and had a contest to find which kid had the most shells. The bus met them at the dock. Ted was content with his job, but was glad to get the last of the children onto the bus. He and Jim had a sandwich at the Pub. Ted got his hundred from Jim and went up to the inn to plan the next leg of his trip.

CHAPTER FOUR

For the next segment of his trip, Ted made plans to visit his old pal Jake Russell. Jake and his wife Kim had a cabin on Bobcat Lake. This was just seven miles west of Wells. His plan was to take the bus to Wells and then attempt to get a ride to Bobcat Lake. If he did not get a ride, he had to hike the last seven miles to the lake. He was strong and athletic and did not object to that.

When Ted left the Kemps, he made a stop in Bath at the Whale Grill. The kids he swam with at Frog Pond were quick to recommend the Whale Grill as the best spot in Bath for a sandwich, snacks and soft drinks. He got a can of coke and a box of cupcakes to take on the bus trip. At the Whale Grill he met a man **called** Brad. Brad came to the Whale Grill to grab a sandwich while his truck was in the shop for a lube job. As Brad ate his sandwich, Ted had a chat with him. It was a stroke of luck for **both** of them that they met at just that time.

Brad was in a bind. He had a contract with the state to take a pile of gravel and stone to a project in Wells. He was all set for the trip when he had a bit of rotten luck. The man who was to help him had a sudden fall and broke his leg. **Without** his assistant, Brad was in distress. Ted told Brad that he was glad to assist him if Brad would give him a ride to Wells. That was fine with Brad. Ted gave Brad a lift with the gravel and stone. With Ted's help, Brad did accomplish his job and met his contract, and Ted got a lift to Wells.

On the trip, Ted kept up an endless chitchat and told Brad of his travels. He told of the kit fox on the bus, the swim with the kids at Frog Pond, and his attempt to nap with the cat at the Kemps. Brad was fed up with the long gabfest and glad when they got to Wells. Ted was glad to save the bus fare.

To express his thanks for the ride, Ted

gave Brad the rest of the cupcakes.

It was **about** five when Brad and Ted got to Wells. Ted had not yet had lunch. With much thanks for the ride, he left Brad and went to find **food**. He had to get in shape for his long hike to Bobcat Lake. He had to admit he was lost in Wells.

He made a stop at a drugstore for a coke. At last, he came to Big Tom's Sandwich Shop and went in. Big Tom himself was at the stove. A cute **girl** got him a plate of fresh spinach salad, a chicken sandwich, and a glass of milk. Ted **thought** the **girl looked** fantastic in her spotless white dress and pink cap. Her name was Liz.

Ted told Liz and Big Tom that he was on his way to Bobcat Lake. Big Tom left his skillet to recommend that Ted take the old ox path. The ox path was a wide lane made for oxen and mules to drag logs to the mill. It was just five miles long, not the seven miles given on the map. The path had no traffic, but it was **full** of twists and bends, and a man could get lost if he set off at dusk. Tom gave Ted the address of the Wells Inn and told him that it was best to spend the **night** at the inn. Then he could get up with the sun and set off fresh.

Ted had a long chat with Liz. She was quite **nice**. He was timid, but at last got up the spunk to express himself and ask her for a date. At that, Big Tom got a bit indignant. He told Ted that the cute **girl** with the blond **hair** did just happen to be his wife. Big Tom objected to Ted's bold tactics. Ted did not wish to offend Liz, and did not relish the prospects of a conflict with her husband.

Ted was upset and made a quick exit. He went to the inn and slept well in spite of the fact that he did not get a date with Liz.

Ted got up at seven and had a quick shave and a scrub in the bathtub. He had codfish cakes, bran muffins, and eggs at the inn. The man at the desk made a crude map to help him find the ox path. The map had no compass rose and was a maze of lines and ink dots that Ted did not quite grasp. Ted went to the shop next to the inn and got some snacks in a plastic bag for the trip. With straps and rope he slung his bag on his back and set off for Bobcat Lake. It was a grand time for a brisk hike, and he sang a soft tune to himself as he strode off to the west. He felt glad to be **free** and by himself.

Before long he came to a big red stone like the red dot at the bottom of his map. A wide lane led from the stone, much like the line on his map, and he chose to take that lane. He felt that Bobcat Lake must be at the end of the lane.

In time, the wide lane had shrunk to a thin path. At last it came to a sudden end in a thick stand of pine saplings. Ted sat on a log to adjust his pack and assess the problem. He felt the best method was to attempt to connect up with that big red stone. That would establish his exact site on the map. He went back, but the path was full of zigzags with side paths that would vanish in thickets. Which path to take? His map did not help. The upshot was that he was lost and had to admit it. It was maddening, but he would not let himself panic. In a mere whim, he chose a random path that led to a splendid, wide glade with a fresh, cold spring. He was glad to unstrap his pack, unbutton his jacket, and rest a while. He had a long drink from the spring and then had a fine picnic lunch on the snacks from his plastic bag. Then he fell back on a blanket of soft moss to doze in the sun.

Ted sank back on that soft blanket of moss intending to doze for just a while, but he woke to a crimson sunset. He was upset with himself for such a long nap. He did not relish the prospect of spending the **night** by himself in the brush. He got up to adjust his pack, button up his jacket and finish his travels. Then, to add to his distress, he could smell a hint of smoke in the soft wind that swept in from the west. It sent a chill up his spine to think he had to combat a brush fire. In a **moment** a second gust of wind bore a distinct smell of smoke to his nostrils. He felt he must not panic. He had gotten himself lost. The problem now was to find a **way** to get **out** of this mess. He chose to think the whiff of smoke came from a campfire. Less than a mile to his left a thin plume of smoke rose from the brush. His best hope was that the smoke came from an encampment. With that wishful thinking, he set off intent on finding that campfire.

He had to accustom himself to the diminishing **light** as he crept **through** the brush in quest of the fire. He came to a soft path and made more rapid progress with less crashing in the brush. At last he did find an encampment in a grove of aspens. A small fire sent up its plume of smoke. Ted crept close and hid in the shade of a pile of logs to assess his problem and plot his next step. The flames lit up the grove. A man sat next to the fire with an ax at his side. His wide hat brim hid all but his chin and the tip of his nose. He rose from time to time to attend to the fire. He would take twigs from a basket, toss them on the fire and poke up the flame. The blaze and the smoke cast the man in a devilish, crimson haze. With the sunset, a chill fell on the land, and Ted felt the damp cold in his bones. He had to get close to that fire and drive off the chill. Ted could not be timid. He was not content to sit for long in that log pile. He could be the next victim of a bandit or a madman, but it was time for bold and uncommon tactics. In an instant he made up his mind. He left the shade of the log pile, wet his lips, and spoke up.

When Ted spoke the man sprang up. He spun to glare at the log pile and made a grab for his ax. The wide brim of his hat was at a tilt to obscure all but his nose and chin. With his back to the fire he was like a caveman with a devilish aspect in the crimson haze of smoke. He kept his legs bent, catlike, as if to spring. For a moment Ted felt he had made a mistake and should rush back into the wild brush to escape the insane madman and his ax.

Just then a gust of wind swept the man's hat off to expose his entire **face**. With a gasp, Ted **saw** that the man at the campfire was his oldtime classmate Jake Russell! Ted was safe at last. He was fit to explode. With a yell he sprang into the campsite. He ran to Jake for a handshake and a hug. It was a complete shock to Jake. All he did was stand and gape. Ted had not told of his plan to visit, and Jake did not expect him. It was quite a scare to Jake to have a wild man yell and rush at him from the pile of logs.

When Jake could compose himself, he was just as glad as Ted that he had not hit him with his ax. Ted had to update Jake on the happenings of his **own** life, to inquire of Jake's life and to compare facts. He told Jake of his hike from Wells with his handmade map, of the winding and branching of the ox path that did confuse him until he was lost. It was just blind luck for him to find Jake at his campsite.

Jake then did invite Ted to visit in his lakeside cabin. His wife was off on a trip, but would be home in a **day** or **two**. While she was off, he came to complete a job cutting brush for the state. Jake gave Ted a big plate of his homemade grub and a hot drink. Ted shed his jacket and hung it next to the fire to drive off the dampness and chill. When it got late, they crept close to the campfire to escape the cold, and slept. They would postpone more chatting until sunrise.

Ted was grateful to Jake and to the fate that led him to Jake's campsite in the midst of this vast brush thicket.

Jake had a contract with the state to attend to a plot of **forest** land in his upstate district. His job was to inspect and prune the big pines and thin the brush. This was to expose the crop of saplings to more sunshine and to suppress fungus and mold. He had to be careful of the saplings. His job in the **forest** was not just cosmetic; it was an economic asset to the state and a help for the wildlife, as well. With the cutting complete, he would collect the twigs and brush, compile a big volume and set fire to it. He had to be careful not to ignite a fire that would consume the entire **forest** and level the landscape. To compensate him, the state gave him cash and let him have the big logs for himself. He cut and split these logs to stove size and made a pile of them. When the lake froze he had his mule drag them on a big sled to the shed next to his home. Jake was grateful for the job, and glad to get the logs for his stove.

Ted and Jake woke at sunrise. To finish his job, Jake had more brush and logs to cut, and Ted was glad to assist him. Jake had to advise him on the method to prune. In the end they did contrive a plan to combine jobs: Jake would prune and Ted would collect and rake. With this plan they got the plot trim and shipshape. The sun shone to infiltrate the forest and infuse fresh life into the plants. It was ten when the last log was split. With the job complete, they ran to the pond to freshen up with a quick dip.

When they left the camp they had to extinguish the fire. Jake had made the fire inside a big concave pit with a line of stones at the bottom and on all sides. He had let the fire subside, but the bottom of the pit was still a hotbed of red ash. A gust of wind could ignite the ash to explode into flames and invite a brush fire. They had to bring **water** from the pond to drench the fire pit. Only when the last telltale red ash was wet could they assume it was safe for them to **leave** the campsite.

When Ted and Jake left the campsite,

they had to hike more than a mile to get to the lake. Jake was quick to invite Ted to visit, and Ted was most **grateful**. Jake led the hike. Ted kept close and did not attempt to explore side paths. As long as he was with Jake he was not apt to get lost. He had to admire Jake for his wisdom of the **forest** and the wildlife. Jake was extreme in his wish to upgrade the state of the **forest**. He could not excuse the careless mistakes of those who would misuse or pollute the landscape.

Jake had hid his skiff in the brush at the lakeshore. They slid the skiff into the **water** and got in to cross the lake. It was not a long trip. The homesite that Jake and his wife chose was on the west shoreline of the lake. When they came close to the shore, Jake sat up and gave a yell. A flag was hung on the cabin flagpole which let him assume that his wife was home from her trip to Wells. He sprang from the skiff and ran to her for a big hug and kiss. Ted was left to bring in the skiff. He slid it up on land and **tied** its rope to a stump. Then he came up to the cabin and met Jake's wife. Her name was Kim.

Kim had a **friend** with her.

Kim's **friend** was Rose Sanchez. She and Kim had been classmates and best pals in the seventh grade. Then her dad got a job to administrate a plant in Manhattan, and she and her mom and dad left Wells. Kim had **trouble** in **school** with **reading**, spelling, and math. Rose would assist her when she could, and Kim could attribute most of her **school** accomplishments to the help she got from Rose. Kim's **schooling** was incomplete, but she did demonstrate a fine talent in **art**. She went on to **art school** and got jobs to illustrate texts for children. From time to time she sold her handmade notes and valentines in shops. Her craft did not compensate her well, but it did contribute to the cost of things when she and Jake got the cabin on Bobcat Lake.

Then, more than five **years** from the time she left, Rose made a trip to Wells with her dad. At that same time, Kim was in Wells to get things for the cabin. They met in Wells and had a long lunch. In the end, Kim got Rose to hop in the van and drive with her to Bobcat Lake. They had much to share and had to make up for lost time.

Jake and Kim sat in the sun on the lakeshore and drank lemonade with Ted and Rose. Jake told them the anecdote of Ted's attack on his campsite. He was just glad that he could recognize Ted in time not to dispose of him with his ax. It was fun to tell of it, but it was not such a joke at the time. Jake felt it was kind of Ted to go **out** of his **way** to spend a bit of his trip time with him and his wife.

Ted was grateful to them for letting him visit **their** home. He was more than glad to share his visit with Rose.

Jake and his wife had a long chat with Ted and Rose as they sat on the shore of the lake. At sunset, Kim went in to fix **dinner**, and Jake lit a fire in the stove. Ted and Rose went for a promenade **along** the shore.

Kim had set up a cot for Rose in the loft, and Jake was at a loss to find a spot for Ted within the confines of his small cabin. He had left his big tent at his campsite. His plan was to set up his pup tent, but chipmunks had got into it, and the canvas was **full** of holes. In the end Jake had to designate the van as the spot for Ted. He flung a strip of rug and a felt pad on the flat bed of the van, and Kim gave him blankets and a quilt to put on top of that. It made a fine bed for Ted. There was a mild smell of gas to infiltrate the **air** of the van but no monoxide fumes. Ted would be safe in the van, and was glad not to discommode the Russells in **their** small cabin.

Kim made a fine **dinner** of chicken dumplings and spinach salad. She let Rose distribute the plates and cups. They all had a glass of white wine with their **dinner** to consummate their new and old friendships. They sat for quite a while at the fireside and then went off to bed. Ted crept off to his confinement in the van. It was snug in the van, and he was glad to escape from the cold of the night. With the soft quilt up to his chin, the smell of gas fumes in his nostrils, and the enchantment of Rose in his mind, he fell asleep.

It had **been** an active **day** for Ted, and he slept well until a soft *tap, tap, tap* woke him. It came from the side of the van next to his bed. There was an oppressive stillness in the **night** which gave him a scare and sent a chill up his spine. He froze in his bed, a captive in the van. Then, in a while, *tap, tap, tap,* more intensive this time. At last he sat up and gave a yell, his objective to get the *tapping* to shut up and buzz off. With that, the *tap, tap, tap* did stop. Then a soft tone spoke the name, "Rose."

It was Rose! With that, Ted flung off the quilt, sprang up, and got his **clothes** on. He slid from the van and met Rose on the path that led from the cabin. She told him she felt bad that he had to hole up in that oppressive, cold van while she had a snug cot in the hut. Ted told her she was kind to be so attentive, but he would get more rest if she did not wake him up like that. But he was glad she came. He told her he had slept well, and she must not fret. It was a cold **night**. He held her close and she clung to him as he led her to the cabin. Then, as he left her at the gate, she gave him a quick kiss and ran in. Ted went back to the van but was pensive, thinking of that attractive Rose. He did doze off from time to time, but Rose was still on his mind.

CHAPTER FIVE

It was just sunrise, and the sky was a pale pink when Ted met Rose at the shore of the lake. He sat beside her to resume the chat they had when she came to wake him in the van. Rose was a bit shy. She felt it was stupid for her to behave like that, and went on to describe why she woke him in the van. The Russell's did not expect her to visit, and she did not like to deprive him of his bed in the cabin. She felt she was to blame for why he was in that cold van. She went on and on, and then she began to cry.

Ted was silent to let her finish before his reply. He had to remind her that the Russell's did not expect him and that his visit was just as sudden as hers.

"You must not cry," he said, "But when you made that metallic *tap, tap, tap* on the side of the van, I confess it did scare me. I had to presume that it was someone trying to pry open the van. I did try to yell but my lips were dry. Then when you spoke, I began to relax. You were kind to think of me." With that they both began to smile. He gave her a hug, and they set off hand in hand for a **stroll** beside the lake.

For their sunrise **stroll** they set off on a lane that led into a pine grove behind the cabin. The lane became a thin path which came to an end in an open, sunlit glade. They sat to rest beside a tranquil spring-fed pond, with no other humans to invade this remote spot. It was late in the month of April and the wild iris were in blossom on the banks of the pond. Sumac and locust saplings bent as if to drink and cast their shapes to reflect on the pond. A shy thrush sang its flute solo from a pine branch just beyond the pond, and from time to time the grunt of a bull frog rose from the bog. A spry chipmunk ran zig-zig in frantic quest, and a timid rabbit came to nibble fresh blades of grass. Ted told Rose that this secret haven was to belong just to them. Rose did not respond but did not resist as he bent to brush her lips with his. He held her close beside him for a moment. Then she had to remind him that the Russell's would be up by this time. It would not be polite to ignore their hosts, so she told him they must go. Ted began to protest with the hope to prolong this sublime moment. But this was no time to debate. Rose got up to go and they set off to resume their hike. It was just before seven and the sun was well up by the time they got to the cabin.

Ted and Rose were hungry from their hike. They had bacon and eggs, bagels and milk with Jake and Kim at the picnic bench in the sunshine. Ted told them of their hike and of the dandy pond with the grassy bank and wild iris. Ted went on to propose that Jake and Kim should have time to themselves. To accomplish this he and Rose would take the skiff for a picnic lunch on the lake. Jake did not object to the plan. He was happy to have time to finish projects in his cabin. But he was savvy to his old buddy. He could detect that his plan was a flimsy excuse for Ted to be with Rose. They all went inside to tidy up the cabin and fix a picnic lunch.

Then Jake went with them to prepare the skiff.

Jake had life vests to equip them for the trip. The lake was **deep** and quite chilly, and in the springtime sudden squalls were frequent. Ted was to beware of sudden gusts to prevent an upset. Jake told them to try Sandy Cove as a cozy picnic site. He gave a sly wink, and told Ted to protect Rose from wild rodents and evil snakes. Ted and Rose were a bit clumsy getting into the skiff with the picnic basket, a poncho, and swim things, but they set off with happy prospects. Ted felt equal to the demands of his tiny craft. He chose to pretend he was the pilot of the Golden Dragon with Rose as his regal Dragon Lady.

Ted and Rose were in a happy frame of mind when they left the shore to glide off onto the open lake beyond. The sky was sunny and the lake was tranquil. The only waves were the tiny frills the skiff left behind in its wake. Sandy Cove was close by. They were to go just beyond the stone jetty and then cross the lake to the cove.

To accomplish a crossing was no problem unless a squall came up. In that case they were to make for shore and let the wind subside. It would be insane to try to cross the lake in a squall. The lake could get ugly, and a big wave or eddy could upset a flimsy skiff. Ted was told to study the sky to try to predict the winds.

Ted kept close to land and made fine progress to the end of the jetty. He let the skiff drift from time to time to relax. They sang songs and told of their moms and dads and the homes they came from. They went on to describe the silly fun they had as kids, and to share their problems. Rose said she had a strong desire to get back to Wells, and Ted felt he had to escape from Webb Hill.

They made fine progress to the end of the jetty and made the crossing to Sandy Cove with no problem. It was a most happy trip. They slid the skiff up on the shore and got set for the picnic.

Ted got the picnic basket and his swim trunks from the skiff. Rose flung the poncho open on a grassy spot close to the shoreline and began to distribute the equipment for lunch. She did her best to improvise a tidy, dressy setting for their picnic dining. She even went into the brush to collect wild blossoms and ivy to decorate her picnic lunch. Ted was hot from the lake crossing and was intent on a dip in the lake. He went to a remote spot in the dense brush to slip into his trunks while Rose was setting up the picnic. He made a mad dash into the lake with such a jumbo belly flop that it sent waves up onto the shore. Rose lost no time getting into the lake with him, but made a more ladylike entry. It was chilly but refreshing and relaxing. Ted was protective of Rose and told her not to go beyond her depth, but he was to find that she swam so well that she put him to shame. Ted was then content to manipulate himself in the **water** as best he could. He did try to compensate and impress her with an acrobatic stunt. The result was more comical than impressive. He was no hero, but to Rose he was a brave, attractive, enchanting hunk.

Ted was a fine athlete and was president of the Webb Hill Acrobat Club. His vanity and pride drove him to demonstrate his body skills for the benefit and amazement of Rose. He was not aware that Rose was an acrobat with the Big **Apple Circus** in Manhattan. She was to compete in the next **Festival** of Acrobats in Atlanta.

A massive pine **tree** rose from the bank next to the shore and sent a big branch over the lake. To Ted that branch would constitute a lofty trapeze for him to demonstrate his acrobatics. He did not hesitate. In a moment he was up in the pine with a strong grip on the branch. He swung five or six times, and then did a flip into the lake. In his estimate of such a difficult stunt, his mistake was to miscalculate the altitude of the branch. He hit the lake with a clumsy splash. The act was an absolute and dramatic flop. It was truly comical. Rose was not impolite and did not ridicule him. She even swam to him to congratulate him on his skill and compliment him on his brave attitude. He did not injure himself more than a tiny cut on his hand. Rose put an adhesive on that and gave him plenty of pity. Ted felt it was wise to abandon the trapeze act. The only significant effect on him was to compromise his dignity and deflate his ego.

CHAPTER SIX

They had a refreshing swim with lively games and swimming stunts. Rose was a skillful and tireless athlete. When they had finished the trapeze act and random games, they sat on the sandy shore. The lake was chilly, but the sun shone hot to dry them almost instantly. After the eventful swim, they had a long chat with much wishful thinking on the subject of home. Rose had a fondness for **Maine**, and just lately felt she would like to resume her life in Wells. Ted had the strongest desire to escape from Webb Hill. Besides that, he began to think his prime requirement in life was to be close to Rose. Their plans had the same objective. It was not likely that they would both land in Wells, but it was not hopeless. It was useless to make such plans at this time. It was the stuff wishes were made of, but it did provide vast amusement for them on the picnic. They were supremely happy as they sat on the sunny shore.

Ted was sensitive to the sun and his skin had taken on a distinct pinkish tone. He had to be careful, so he went to dress. By this time they were hungry, so they went to the picnic lunch that Rose had so carefully set up. The poncho kept the dampness from the grass, but did not repel the ants. While Rose and Ted were at the lake, swinging from the branches and basking in the sun, a colony of ants were visiting their lunches and silently demolishing their sandwiches. This was to provide no amusement to Ted and Rose, but it did not dampen their appetites. The ants were as hungry as they, and it would be selfish to deny them a scrap. With skillful brushing they got rid of the ants, and ate their sandwiches and refreshments as blithely as if the ants had been invited. It was just an episode in their eventful picnic.

When Ted and Rose and the ants had finished the picnic, they dunked the dishes in the lake and stashed them in the picnic basket. They folded the poncho and stuffed it in the skiff with the basket. Then they inspected their picnic site for trash and ended by wishing Sandy Cove a fond farewell. They had been extremely happy on this picnic and were thankful for the contentment it had given them.

They were reminded that Jake had instructed them to scan the sky and sniff the wind before setting off across the lake. It was hazy, hot, and humid, but the sky in the west had taken on a dull, slate shade. Ted and Rose did not like the ashen shade of the sky in the west and were reminded of the sudden squalls Jake had described. But they felt the stillness was a hopeful omen. A soft puff of wind drifted across the cove. They discussed the subject and finally dismissed Jake as a wimpy pessimist and scoffed at his ultra safe attitude. A tiny puff of wind presented no difficulty. Their trip to Sandy Cove had been accomplished with no distress, and they predicted that the trip back would be as blissful.

They got into their life vests, bid Sandy

Cove a fond farewell, and set off across the lake. It was a fine trip until they left the protected cove and got into the open lake. By then the entire sky was dusky and ugly, and the wind had suddenly shifted. Waves bashed into the tiny skiff and splashed **over** its sides. They attempted to bale, but it was useless, and before long the skiff was filled.

A big wave lifted the picnic basket and tossed it into the lake. At last a mammoth wave crashed into the skiff, upset it, and dumped Ted and Rose in the lake. For a moment they were filled with panic as the skiff drifted off, bottom side up. But they were skilled swimmers, and their blessed life vests helped to hold them up. They swam to the skiff and clung to it, adrift and buffeted by the angry waves. The squall passed promptly. It lasted only moments and ended as suddenly as it began. They **righted** the skiff and were happy to find the **oars** still inside. With their hands they sloshed the **water** to empty it and got it as dry as they could. They finished the trip, sodden, mussed, and chilled to the bone. They were also disgusted with themselves. They wished they had trusted Jake and not risked their lives in such careless abandon.

Ted and Rose came ashore dampened but happy. Jake tactfully asked if they were aware of the squall that so destructively swept the lake a while ago. Ted told Jake that their trip was fatefully disrupted by that squall. The wind had unexpectedly swelled to an impressively angry tempest. He told of their helplessness as the waves crashed relentlessly on the skiff, upset it and left them thrashing ineffectively in the waves as the skiff drifted off. For a moment they felt hopelessly lost. Then Rose told how Ted manfully swam to the skiff and skillfully **righted** it. She spoke regretfully of the loss of the picnic basket. She would replenish the picnic things when they went to Wells. She related that they spent their time at Sandy Cove blissfully and restfully, romping childishly in the lake and chatting endlessly. They lunched on the tastefully prepared sandwiches, the poncho attractively draped with wild blossoms and entwined with strands of ivy. Jake instinctively suspected that the ivy she mindlessly collected was **poison** ivy, but he did not say so.

It ended well, but Jake scolded Ted for not attending to the lessons of the sky. His carelessness could have cost them their lives.

When Ted and Rose had a hot bath and got into dry clothes they were able to relax with the Russells. A gentle drizzle had set in, and the dampness and puddles kept them inside. Ted collected dry sticks and twigs to kindle a fire in the grate. Jake opened a bottle of soda, and they all sat at the fireside. The Russells got a big chuckle out of Ted's trapeze act at Sandy Cove. Ted embellished the tale of their battle with the tempest and their struggle to save the skiff as it drifted off. He made it seem that they were truly lucky to be alive.

When Kim called them to the table, Rose distributed the plates, and Ted lit the candles. Before they ate, they clasped hands and gave thanks for the blessings of old chums and happy lives. Jake and Kim had prepared an ample menu consisting of chicken and dumplings, tossed salad, muffins with plum jam, and apple crisp. When they had finished, they got up from the table and settled on the sofa in front of the fire. They had a fine time discussing their past lives and bringing themselves up to date.

As they sat before the fire, Ted described his home in Webb Hill, his mom and dad, and his job at the mill. He was fond of the simple life but chose not to spend his life, cradle to grave, in Webb Hill. To help make up his mind, he elected to take time off to travel. He did not tell them that he broke up with his gal. Rose and Kim had been classmates in Wells. Rose liked Manhattan, but Wells was still home to her.

Kim's mom and dad came to Boston from Ireland and settled in Wells. Her dad was accomplished on the fiddle and the flute. With his Irish tunes he provided musical amusement for the patrons of the local pubs. Jake came from Bath where his dad had cattle on a small plot of land. Jake was in the navy for a while and then came to Wells to take a job with the state.

Jake met Kim at a bible study class. They dated a long time before their wedding.

By the time the fire had dwindled to a rosy red ash, they could barely hold their lids open and could not stifle their yawns. The frenzy of that lake squall had taken its toll on Ted and Rose. It was time to shuffle off to bed.

They all slept late and awoke well rested. The men inspected the skiff for defects as a result of the upset in the squall. There was no significant defect, but the impact of the waves had made a tiny split in one of the planks. They fixed the split, flushed off the mud and sand, and set the skiff in the sun to dry. When it was dry Jake got his fishing tackle and they spent a lazy time drifting along the shore. They didn't get any fish; it was mostly just the fun of old pals relaxing in the sun.

While the men tended to the skiff and fished, Kim and Rose had a splendid time inspecting old photos and recalling the games of basketball and baseball, the dates they had, the picnics, and the proms.

They all met for lunch and had a swim while the sun was still hot. They discussed their plans, hopes and prospects for the **future**. Jake had his job with the state and Kim had her job in Wells. They intended to settle in their cabin on the lake and make it their home.

Rose wished she could live in Wells with her old **friends**, but that was difficult with her family in Manhattan. Ted began to recognize the problems of a vagabond but still wished to travel a bit more. He even began thinking of a trip to Manhattan to visit Rose.

The next **day**, Jake and Kim had to go to Wells to get equipment for the cabin. Ted wished to get on with his trip, and Rose had to go back to Manhattan with her dad. And so, the next day they all got into the van and set off for Wells.

They got to Wells just before eleven. Rose and Ted went to a craft shop and got a picnic basket for the Russells. This was a gift to **replace** the basket they lost in the lake. Then, as an extra gift, they got an insulated case for bottles or cans on trips or picnics. It came complete with plastic cups and plates. The Russells were grateful for such a useful and handy gift and thanked them profusely. When they had finished their shopping they bid farewell to Ted and Rose and drove back to Bobcat Lake.

Ted went with Rose and met her dad at the hotel. Mr. Sanchez was tall and solid with a prominent chin and flashing eyes. He was dressed trimly and tastefully in immaculate clothes, quite in contrast to Ted's rumpled travel clothes. He was a commanding and cold figure with a bone crushing handshake. The effect was to intimidate Ted.

Mr. Sanchez told them that his company was sending him back to handle the Wells district. He was also to be assistant to the president of the company. He would have to bring his family back to Wells. Rose was ecstatic at the prospect of coming back to her old home. She told her dad that Ted was jobless and on a trip, but would like to live in Wells. Ted was astonished that Rose made such a bold statement. Mr. Sanchez did not commit himself, but told Ted to complete his trip and call him if and when he got back to Wells. His plant was expanding and he intended to hire more staff.

When they were alone Ted was indignant and asked Rose why she had told that fantastic fable. What made her think that he would like to get a job with her dad in Wells? Rose blushed and responded that she did assume Ted would like to settle in Wells. She did hope he would.

Mr. Sanchez had to revisit his company before he left for Manhattan. He had problems to study and methods to recommend for expanding the volume of their product. He invited Ted to go along with him. It was polite of Mr. Sanchez to include him. Ted had not expected this but was grateful for the kindness. He went along, and while Mr. Sanchez did his thing Ted spent time studying the crates and boxes used to pack and ship the products. It re-minded him of his job in his dad's box shop back in Webb Hill. He had a fine chat with the shop foreman. By the end of the visit Ted was much impressed with the plant. He began to respect Mr. Sanchez and even liked him.

After his visit with Mr. Sanchez, Ted went back to the gift shop next to the craft shop. Rose was flying back to Manhattan with her dad the next day, and he had to get something for her. He was not aware of what she would like, but he had to get something. He did not wish to get mushy, but it had to be something with a sentiment and a hint of times to come. He asked the lady at the gift shop to advise him, but she was no help. It had to be something to welcome her back home. He contemplated getting a Wells pennant, but he dismissed that; she would have one of those from **school**. Then he recalled that she liked plants and a **garden**. So he got her a packet of **seeds**. They would fit in her handbag and be on hand to plant when she got back home. It was not a lavish gift but it had sentiment and hope for establishing her home in Wells. Also, he selfishly hoped he could share the gift with her when she planted them. He got five packets in case she did not like one. The lady put them in a tiny gift box to include his note, "**See** you in your **garden** in June."

Ted went to the plane with them to bid them a fond farewell. He felt lonely with a pang of sadness as the plane lifted off and blended into the distant sky. He was left alone to plan the next segment of his trip. With the map of the United States before him he rattled off such romantic names as Boston, Washington, Baltimore, Atlanta, Buffalo, Reno, El Paso, Dallas, Cleveland, Honolulu, and more. There were endless possible travel sites. He had to chuckle that he could even be a hobo in Hoboken.

But the prospect of travel was less thrilling than before. He had to confess that he missed Rose. If he did not have Rose at his side, his life was incomplete and his travels less satisfying. As he left Wells and set off for Boston, his step was less brisk, and his pack was a bit more oppressive.

He was inclined to think that before long, he would end his travels in Wells.